Sleepless NIGHTS

Marie Zitnansky is also the author of the book

Doctor's Life Beyond – True Story with Research into Life After Death

Sleepless NIGHTS

POEMS EXPRESSING LOVE, SORROW FOR LOST LOVE, AND HOPE FOR PEACE

Poems of Love, Sorrow, and Hope

M.J. ZITNANSKY

Rushmore Press LLC
www.rushmorepress.com
1 888 733 9607

Sleepless Nights

Copyright © 2019 by M.J. Zitnansky.

ISBN   Softcover   978-1-950818-02-0

All rights reserved. No part of this publication may be reproduced, distributed, or transmitted in any form or by any means, including photocopying, recording, or other electronic or mechanical methods, without the prior written permission of the author, except in the case of brief quotations embodied in critical reviews and certain other noncommercial uses permitted by copyright law.

Printed in the United States of America.

In loving memory of my late husband.
I dedicate these poems to my children –
Martin, Daniel and Monica. To my grandchildren.
To Grace, my daughter-in-law and Martin Dykstra, my son-in-law.

Contents

To My Beloved Husband 1
When We Walked The Road Together. 2
Why Did You Do This To Me? 3
We All Miss You. 4
I'll Be There 5
I Love You All 6
Love From Above 7
Who Are You? 8
The Secret 9
Love is Never Lost 10
Happiness and Sorrow 11
Death Can't Steal the Memories of You 12
I Remember You. 13
I Can Never Forget You 15
On Love and Pain 16
The Message. 17
The Longing of the Soul 18
The Passion of the Soul. 19
The Dream 20
You Are Near 21
Life is Like a River. 22
It Is Just a Word the Doctors Say 23
The Tears in the Lines 24
Being Together 25

Anam Cara	26
On Sleepless Nights	28
On Sorrow	29
The Lightning	30
God's Creation	31
God is the Creator	33
God's Wisdom	34
Life's Journey	35
The Lonely Mother	37
God's Grace	38
Our Father	39
God's Rules	40
In the Steps of St. Francis' Prayer	41
We Need a Healer	42
My Lord	43
Prayer to the Trinity	44
God's Plan	45
God's Love	46
Longing for God's Love	47
The Longing	48
What a Great Love	49
On Love	50
Stop Fighting	51
God and His People	52
Preachers	53
The Designer	54

God's Will	55
The Power of God	56
God's Nature	57
All Religions	58
Two Ways	59
The Prayer in the Garden	60
On Power	61
The One Who Always Was	62
The Calvary Hill	63
The Judgment Day	64
On Joy	65
Seen and Unseen	66
Mother's Plea	67
Ava	68
My Grandchildren	69
Parent's Advice	70
Drowning	71
The Spoiled Son	73
To My Sister-in-Law	74
The Stepmother	75
The Orphan	77
The Lavender Bush	78
Picking Blueberries	79
Clearing in the Woods	80
The Deer is Coming	81
Going Fishing	82

The Fisherman and the Fish 83
The Outdoors 84
The Well in the Woods 85
The Invasion 86
The Time I Don't Forget 87
Three Travelers from a Distant Land 88
The Enemies 89
People Of Mutual Love 91
The Hate 92
Young People Need Direction 93
The Oasis 94
Rest Body and Soul 95
On Metamorphosis 96

To My Beloved Husband

God let you live and prosper,
Then He let you be with me.
He let you die and took you home,
But you took with you a part of me.

You love me, I know, and the love is mutual
And this is the way it will always be.
When the father took you home
He did not think of the rest of me.

The rest of me is struggling to be proper.
I wish you would be with me.
The Father will call and take me home,
But only when it is time to go for me.

I have your children; their hearts are pain-filled.
They show respect and love to me.
I love them too but they left my home.
I know that one day you will be back for me.

To know Father's plan would be helpful,
But He doesn't reveal it to you or me.
I know that He wants to bring me to His home
And that we will be together always, you and me.

This poem is also published in my book
"Doctor's Life Beyond."

When We Walked The Road Together

When we walked the road together
I had you by my side.
Then Father called you home
And I lost my joy and pride.

You left me in pain,
Crying and alone.
I sensed the love you sent me from above,
I knew I had to get up and go.

My pain is greater than I can bear,
I know you don't want me to cry.
I know you want to be proud of me.
I know I have to get up and try.

When we knew you would be taken away from us,
We did not want to let you go
But it is all in the Father's plan.
These were seeds already sewn.

I try to be good and do good deeds,
To see and not to live as the blind.
You came and told me "Live",
I know that's why I was left behind.

On sleepless nights you come to me,
I know that you are near.
I have to get up and write the rhymes
That you whisper in my ear.

This poem is also published in my book
"Doctor's Life Beyond".

Why Did You Do This To Me?

You were twenty-four when you found me.
You were twenty-four when you fell in love with me.
You were twenty-four when you enchanted me.
You were twenty-five when you doctored me.
You were twenty-six when you married me.
You were twenty-eight when you fled our country with me.
You were twenty-eight when you started a hard life with me.
You were a happy man when you laughed with me.
You were a good doctor when you instructed me.
You were a good husband when you corrected me.
You were a good father when you raised our children with me.
You got ill and you died on me.
Why did you do this to me?

We All Miss You

I think of you during the day,
I think of you during the night.
I think of you when I pray,
You are always on my mind.

I talk about you with our friends,
I write about you in my book.
I see you in my mind,
You are the part of me that God took.

I don't know what it means
But whoever knew you can't forget you.
You have influenced their lives,
There are only a few people like you.

We want to know where you are,
Yet we need to stop the search.
We want to know where you went,
I search for you every day since you left.

I learned about an awesome place
When I started the search for you.
We want to know if you are there,
We want to know what there is to do.

Let us know how to find you,
We are searching everywhere.
We want to know about that place
And one day we all will be there.

I'll Be There

When I finish my earthly journey
And fulfill what you want me to do,
I hope to be able to rest a while
And send thanks for it to you.

You inspire me and give me strength
To do what has to be done.
There is a lot of work to be finished,
I can only do it one by one.

God's presence among us has to be known,
We have to do work in His name.
We have to protect God's image,
God's image in the world is not the same.

God created Earth and Heaven,
He expends the universe.
We are destroying his creation,
We are hurting ourselves.

I wish I could talk to all the people,
To tell them about what God said.
To remind them what they are made of,
To stop polluting planet Earth.

When I get weary, hold my hand my darling.
I want to find you, so show me where.
And when I accomplish my earthly mission,
Just call my name and I will be there.

I Love You All

Remember the time we were all together?
It was the time before you left;
The time you were still with us.
You were talking to us from your death bed.

You said, "I love you all,
But I did not show it to you enough."
This was from you, your farewell.
This was your last words to us.

If we could only know what awaits us,
We would try to enjoy you more. We trust God with our lives;
We did not know what the future may have in store.

God is the one who gave us life,
And he is the one who can take it away.
But only when we leave this Earth,
Will he show us the place where we will stay?

To understand God's plans is not easy,
We have to be prepared to go away.
We have to make sure we will see each other
In another place with Him one day.

Love From Above

I lost my protector,
I lost my love.
I lost my advisor
And blamed it on one who should be just.

He tried to calm me down
By showing me His love.
I refused to hear Him,
I denied His love in pride.

He continued to love me,
Showing me all the joys in life
While telling me,
"Don't worry; your loved one is alive!"

I lost my loved one
But I got help from above,
Teaching me to trust the creator,
To believe in another life.

I was given a tool,
In the form of a pen
To write down what has happened…

And why I will see my loved one again.

Who Are You?

Who are you, my darling, who are you,
That I can't stop loving you.
I think of you every day.
Who are you? I have no clue.

I remember your smile.
You seem to be with me,
Even if I don't see you
And you don't talk to me.

It is a mystery that I can't solve,
A mystery that started years ago.
Only people that knew you can believe me,
That my love for you continues to grow.

I love you with all my heart and my soul,
You are with me wherever I go.
The walk with you is so peaceful,
I feel a piece of the place that I will one day know.

The Secret

Without a word you went away,
Without a word you left us.
I remember your smiles before you left,
You were the strongest among us.

You were full of energy and had plans.
You were courageous, you were not afraid.
You wanted to live.
The plans for you lay ahead.

Your life was too short for your ambition.
Your destiny was to die, not to excel.
You always wanted to look pretty.
Why you had to leave, who can tell?

The memory of you haunts me,
I never saw you ill.
You had plans, you were busy.
Did God not see your will?

You left your son here to wonder
What happened to his mom.
We were apart, but we were close.
What happened to you can't be undone.

You left with a secret,
The secret stayed with you.
You wanted me to know it
But I was too late for you.

Love is Never Lost

To lose the love of one is painful.
To lose your spouse means to lose half of yourself.
But we are together only
Until death brings us to the end.

We promised when we got married
That we would love each other until death,
But we continue to love our loved ones
Beyond this life and we wonder about that.

The love survives.
Love survives beyond death.
Life goes on,
But love survives all that.

There is a connection
Between the Earth and the universe.
We don't know how to explain it
But we feel the connection here on Earth.

We can see and feel the connection
But we have to be calm and listen.
There is enough proof of the afterlife,
The testimonies about it are written.

People that have died
And came back to earth
Tell us about the wonders of God,
Tell us about the universe.

We should not stop to believe in God,
Because we don't understand.
Because we don't understand the beginning
And we don't understand the end.

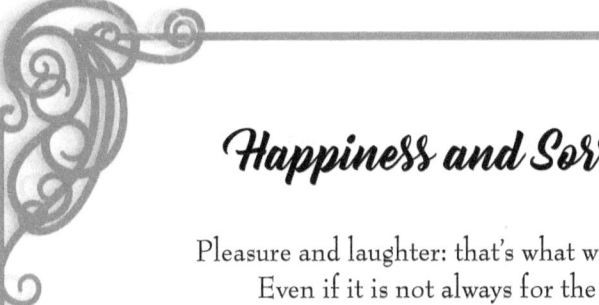

Happiness and Sorrow

Pleasure and laughter: that's what we are after,
Even if it is not always for the best.
To be happy without sorrow,
That is always our quest.

To be happy is not easy,
Sorrow and pain we know best.
If happiness comes our way,
We have to watch what comes next.

Life is never without sorrow,
The sorrow can be more or less.
To be aware what love is
Will secure our happiness.

Death Can't Steal the Memories of You

Death can't steal the memories of you,
Death can't steal the love I feel for you,
Death can't steal the life I had with you,
Death can only steal the feeling of touching you.

We can celebrate the life we shared together,
My heart keeps these memories as treasure,
I remember your smile and tenderness with pleasure,
But the sorrow that you left me has no measure.

I Remember You

In rising of the sun,
I remember you.
For getting up at sunrise,
I admired you.

In watching the sun going down,
I remember you.
When watching the sunset,
I cry for you.

In re-birth of the spring,
I remember you.
When hearing the birds songs,
I want to sing for you.

In seeing the first buds of spring,
I remember you.
By seeing the first flowers in the garden,
I long for you.

In blue skies of summer,
I remember you.
By feeling the warmth of the sun,
I think of you.

In hearing the boats on the lake,
I remember you.
When getting into the boat,
I want to be with you.

In changing colours of the leaves,
I remember you.
Among the beauty of the autumn,
I wait for you.

In seeing the last leaves falling,
I remember you.
Walking across the frozen lake,
I look for you.

When I am tired and need some rest,
I remember you.
The thought of your strength,
Makes me call for you.

I Can Never Forget You

I can never forget you, my darling.
The time I spent with you seems like a dream,
A dream that did not have a happy ending.
I dream about the time now and what it had been.

I dream about your smile,
About your hand holding mine.
I dream about your strength and courage,
What you did and what was not done.

You liked to build, to create, to plant.
You liked to see things grow.
You liked to know about what was going on in the world,
Before I put you six feet below.

The time has passed,
Life is still going.
You told me to live.
My love for you is so deep.

I miss your strength and optimism,
You challenged life and yet accepted death.
You were fighting for your life,
Until death put you to rest.

On Love and Pain

Love is great but it is painful,
It ignites our heart and we are not the same.
Loving people needs a prayer,
To love people is not a game.

Love is patient, love is kind,
But it puts your own ego aside.
Love makes you humble,
Love and pain go side by side.

Love is needed around the whole world.
We should do what love needs.
How we should do this, we don't know yet,
But it should bring the word peace.

To have peace is essential,
It can save you and your friend.
Without peace we could all die.
Wars can destroy us in the end.

The Message

You were the light in this world,
Not letting us look behind, only ahead.
After I put you six feet below,
You showed me the way that I should go.

You told me to live, that you don't want me to cry.
The last time I saw you, that was not good-bye.
I will see you in due time,
But I hope that by then, many years will go by.

I have a lot of work to do on earth,
Sometimes I don't know what I should do first.
There are many tasks that I have to do,
Nobody knows how much of it I owe to you.

The people that you met in this world,
They all adore you and remember what you said.
You were their teacher, you were their guide,
There are many memories that you left behind.

I want to tell them what you showed me,
That there is another life, I'm sure they will agree.
You send a message to my house.
The message is not just for me, it is for all of us.

The Longing of the Soul

My heart is trembling,
I wake up from sleep.
My soul is crying,
The void is so deep.

Calm down my heart
And let me sleep.
Calm my soul,
I need my peace to keep.

My love did not stop flowing,
My tears don't want to dry.
I long for you
Who went up so high.

I know I will see you again,
I know it is not good-bye.
Please calm my soul,
To understand you is worth a try.

I have work to do here.
Your love is like a balm.
I have a duty here,
Please help me stay calm.

I want you to have peace.
Please give me mine.
I have work to do,
Work which takes time.

The Passion of the Soul

Do you know the passion of the soul?
The soul you left alone
In this cruel world?
Do you now hear the cry that in the past you never heard?

There was no crying before you left,
Only a light that shone ahead-
Ahead on a journey of two souls,
The light that was there for both.

Why don't you come to calm my cry?
There are no answers, only why, why, why?
No answers to the questions I ask,
While living without you becomes too much of a task.

You were my pride, you were my sun;
I want you back, but it can't be done.
I live in the past, you left me in shock.
I miss you every day; the days go like a clock.

It's hard to live in this world,
As I try to remember what you said.
I can't leave this world and come,
There is work that has to be done.

The Dream

One night I had a dream,
Long after you left this earth.
I was walking down a street
And a man was walking behind me; I did not see his face.

I did not know what the man wanted from me,
I was wondering what it was all about.
Then the man was walking beside me
But his face was covered with a cloud.

The man gave me enormous peace,
A peace I had not known before.
I was very curious,
I wanted to know more.

The man gave me a feeling of happiness,
He gave me peace, he gave me both.
We were walking on the road,
I was wondering who he was.

We were walking until the end of the road,
Still unsure of who the man was.
Until the man showed his face and I saw you.
I woke up and I knew that I still had to bear my cross.

You Are Near

When I go to places
Where we used to be,
I see you in my mind
And you talk to me.

You help me to know
What should be done.
You are with me again
And I know you are mine.

I know it is just in my head,
I know it is not for real.
I know you are far away,
But I sense that you are near.

Our minds are still connected,
I think of you every day.
My thoughts are all collected,
I want to talk to you again.

Life is Like a River

You are my true love,
The true love that only happens once.
I loved you when I met you,
You were my love at first glance.

I would never have believed
How precious love can be,
If you had not left this world;
If you had not revealed your love to me.

Only God can explain to me
What he instilled in my heart
And how our souls are connected,
How nothing can split them apart.

I can feel you are with me,
Even if I can't see you here.
I think of you every day,
I feel that you are near.

I cannot leave to be with you yet,
I can see you only in my dreams.
I still have a lot to do on this earth.
The life without you is not as easy as it seems.

When I complete my earthly journey,
And my life will take a proper turn,
I want you to come for me then.
I have to complete my life's duty
According to God's Plan.

I will go with you where you want to take me,
I want a tnew life to earn.
Because this life is like a river,
The river with no return.

It Is Just a Word the Doctors Say

I have memories of a life we shared,
Now I can only feel the love
That we had from the start.
I know that you are there.

You lie entombed in sand
But I don't understand,
You can't be dead.
Dead is just a word the doctors say.

I think of you every day,
The thought of you doesn't go away.
You are not dead.
Dead is just a word the doctors say.

I can't forget you and I never will,
I can talk to you and love you still.
You are not dead.
Dead is just a word the doctors say.

When I think of you, I can see your smile
And your soul is with me for a while.
You are not dead.
Dead is just the word the doctors say.

The Tears in the Lines

There are tears in these lines for you,
Who had to go.
There are tears in these lines for me,
Whose love doesn't stop to show.
There are tears in these lines for us,
Whose lives are joined no more.
There are tears in these lines for our children,
Who will never know your love for them
Because it cannot grow.
You told us, "I love you all,
I love you so much with love I could not show.
I love you all, but I have to go."

Being Together

Since I was twenty-four
You were on my side.
When I was twenty-five,
You chose me as your bride.

You taught me your values,
You became my pride.
You became my teacher,
You became my guide.

We went on life's path together,
We shared each other's lives.
We hoped to be together
'Till old age parts us.

I feel like you were stolen from me,
I can't believe that you are gone.
We were supposed to be together,
You should not have left me alone.

I feel like I was cheated,
I feel like I was robbed.
I miss you by my side.
I blame this all on God.

I hope that God will forgive me,
That I blame Him for my loss.
I know you want to be with me,
But I have to bear my cross.

Anam Cara

If you have an Anam Cara,
You better be on guard.
If you have an Anam Cara,
Don't ever let him part.

If you have an Anam Cara,
You never let him go.
You can lose your Anam Cara,
But your love will always grow.

How long can one cry and search for Anam Cara,
The lost soul mate and friend?
No matter how long you search for your Anam Cara,
The search does not seem to end.

I had an Anam Cara,
I lost him on the way.
I lost my Anam Cara
And I am crying every day.

I walk and search for my Anam Cara,
That place is hard to find.
I want to find my Anam Cara.
How could he let me stay behind?

I will look for my Anam Cara
In the place where souls can go and stay.
I will look for my Anam Cara,
In that place one day.

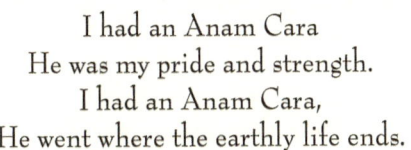

I had an Anam Cara
He was my pride and strength.
I had an Anam Cara,
He went where the earthly life ends.

I will find my Anam Cara,
In that glorious place on my way.
I will find my Anam Cara,
I will join him and there I will stay.

On Sleepless Nights

On sleepless nights I talk to you,
I see your smile's charm.
You dry my eyes, you calm me down,
And let my dreams come.

On sleepless nights I feel the pain
That only you can heal.
I know you love me and I love you,
And that's what brings you near.

How can I stop my tears from coming?
I know you had to go.
I could not stop you, I could not help you.
It just made my love grow.

I never thought we would part this way,
You were so sure and strong.
You never feared; you were never startled.
The way to you is long.

I know I will see you one day again,
I try to be calm.
I talk to you, I pray to you.
I do what has to be done.

I know that you see me from above.
I will see your open door
When God will call me and tell me to come,
And there won't be pain any more.

On Sorrow

There is a sorrow in my heart
That nobody can heal.
I wish I could have you at my side,
I wish that you were here.

There is a sorrow in my heart
That doesn't go away.
My friends are trying very hard
To take that sorrow away.

How long will that sorrow stay with me?
How long will it be in my heart?
I know you had to leave me
But our hearts don't want to part.

God created us in His image,
I hope He loves us the same way.
To love you is a privilege.
I hope your love and mine are the same.

I was told that love is forever,
That it never goes away.
I hope that you will guide me,
From your new home every day.

I hope that God will help me
To heal the sorrow that is still there.
I hope that He will help me find you,
That He will show me where.

The Lightning

Memories are all I have now
Of the days we spent together.
Memories is all I have now
Of your smile, laughter and leisure.

With busy lives that we both had,
I did not know what it all meant
For me to have you by my side,
Until death tore us apart.

I did not know that you could leave me,
I did not know that you would go away.
Away from me, who loved you so much.
I did not know that the sun could become grey.

With busy lives and plans for the future
The lightning came and struck us both.
We tried to get up and recover
From the lightning that struck you most.

The lightning could have killed us both
But I was the one who was spared.
It just struck me and left the scars.
You were the one who was burned.

My life is lonely now without you,
I miss your smile every day.
I miss your guidance through life's sorrows,
I look for you always on my way.

I know you have gone to a better place,
To a better place that I don't know.
I want to find that better place
Where people say souls can go.

God's Creation

God created earth and heaven,
God created you and me.
He gave earth to us as treasure,
Each of us has a destiny.

We think we can do what we want.
We think we can conquer sky.
We think we can change the planet.
We'll pay for it, you and I.

God is King of earth and heaven.
God is King of everything.
He makes new stars and new planets.
He makes every living thing.

Universe is getting bigger.
God is set in His ways.
God has hold of all creation.
He can destroy the human race.

We don't listen to His calling;
We don't listen to His wish.
What we do is most appalling,
How long will God stand all this?

We should listen to His calling,
We should listen to His wish,
We should not change His creation.
We should leave it as it is.

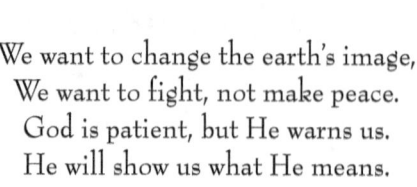

We want to change the earth's image,
We want to fight, not make peace.
God is patient, but He warns us.
He will show us what He means.

God has His rules. God commands us
Not to steal and not to kill.
He teaches us to love each other.
All of us should do His will.

God is the Creator

God, You are the creator of the universe.
God, You are the creator of the world.
God, You created life.
God, You can cause the world to end.

God, You have shown the biochemists
How the human body works.
You have shown how everything blends together,
How our cells integrate.

You showed us, God, how everything has its purpose,
How everything has a design.
God, You are the designer.
God, You are the only one.

We can never deny You, God,
You showed yourself in DNA.
The DNA is like computers
That we are using nowadays.

How can we deny You, God, as a creator,
If science and scriptures share the same path?
Your Son talked to us with authority
About You, God, and about us.

We have denied You God as the creator.
Please forgive us for what we have done.
We will understand all this later,
When science and scriptures will prove to be one.

God's Wisdom

God, Your wisdom is so powerful.
God, your words are so true.
Your Son is so merciful,
He taught us all about You.

Your laws, God, are lifesaving.
Your laws have to be obeyed.
Your laws keep us alive.
We should follow what Jesus said.

The world can expect a disaster,
If we will not keep Your laws.
You are the Lord and creator,
You know where the lawlessness goes.

Lord, you gave us free will,
You don't force us to obey.
All you want from us is to know you
And follow your laws day by day.

Life's Journey

You are born from you mother's womb,
You crawl, stand up and go.
You learn to talk and obey.
Your parents watch as you grow.

You are good and you are naughty,
You have to learn what is right.
You appreciate life's beauty,
You learn that life is hard.

You will laugh and you will be mad,
You may even try to fight.
You will find that the fight is not pleasant.
Will you be bad or good? Only you can make it right.

You will go to school and learn some knowledge,
You will be told to behave.
You will be poor or privileged,
You will learn life's game.

You will be lazy or you will be a doer,
You will procrastinate or move ahead.
You will be poor or you will be wealthy,
You will be happy or you will be condemned.

You will be set on life's journey,
A journey from which you can't go back.
You can only go ahead and stumble,
A journey on which you have to stay on track.

You can learn from what you have seen on your path,
But you can't change what you have done.
What was done can't be undone.
Your life can be dull or you can have fun.

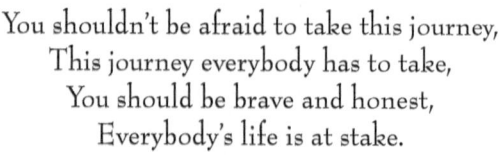

You shouldn't be afraid to take this journey,
This journey everybody has to take,
You should be brave and honest,
Everybody's life is at stake.

When you come to the end of your life's journey,
Don't be afraid to stop and die,
It is everybody's goal in this life,
For life and death is a tie.

The Lonely Mother

Where are you my child?
Your father is dead.
"I love you my son,"
Were the last words your father said.

I want to find you,
My heart is aching,
I want to be with you,
My hands are shaking.

I love you so much,
Why are you not her?
My heart longs for you,
Why are you not near?

You left your father's house,
You did not say where you went.
You left and did not come back,
Where were you sent?

I brought you up,
I kept you from strife,
Why did you leave your home?
I prayed to the One who gave us this life.

I prayed to God the Almighty,
To keep you healthy and safe.
You were too young when you left,
You don't know that your father is in his grave.

I don't know where you went,
I don't know where to find you,
Please hear the cry of my soul,
Let me see again that the sky is blue.

God's Grace

Amazing Grace that God gives us,
The Grace for you and me.
God wants us to be with Him in His house,
He wants it for you and me.

It's Grace to be among His friends,
And Grace our fears relieved.
It is the fear that we won't live,
It is the death we fear.

It's Grace to have our fears relieved,
By God's promises of life.
It's Grace to know that we will live,
The hope for which we strive.

How many times we heard His words,
His words that are our heart's cure.
We must believe in what He said,
We must believe it's true.

There is no fear in our hearts
If the future is not dim.
If we get scared and lose our faith,
We will just think of Him.

Our Father

Our Father, who art in heaven, You are the only One,
Who has the power and whose will has to be done.
We are your children, who don't obey,
We will come to You to be judged one day.

Please Father; protect us from the evil one,
So that only good work on earth can be done.
We have a free will, which leads us astray,
We have the will, which could destroy us one day.

You gave us the rules but we disobey,
You told us what to do, but we are sinning day by day.
We are not sorry for what we have done,
We don't listen to You, but to the evil one.

Let us get the wisdom, Father. Take away our fright.
Teach us not to pollute and how not to fight.
The wisdom and peace will bring us pleasure,
To be with you one day as the last measure.

God's Rules

God made the world,
He made the stars,
All of His creation
He gave to us.

God made the rules
For you and I,
Without His rules
The world will die.

As He is up high
And we are down low,
He shows us the way
That we should go.

Since God is up high
And we are below,
God has the right
To say yes or no.

God has His wish,
God has His ways,
It is not our wish,
These are not our ways.

He is the light,
He is the way,
He is the truth,
We should obey.

He makes new homes
For you and me,
When it is done,
He will say, "Follow Me."

In the Steps of St. Francis' Prayer

Lord, in the steps of St. Francis of Assisi,
Let me sow your love.
Let me disperse the darkness,
Let me see your light.

Lord, let me understand,
To pardon those who want to hurt.
To console the others
And to be consoled at the end.

Lord, there is so much hatred in the word.
Only love can solve it, as St. Francis said.
Lord, there is so much injury that needs to be pardoned.
Only with trust in You we can be safe.

Lord, St. Francis was the instrument of your peace,
The peace that all of us so desperately need.
The injuries and hatred brings us sadness,
And doesn't satisfy the greed.

Lord, only your peace can save the world,
As St. Francis said.
And as for dispersing darkness, we need light,
So with dying we can be born to eternal life.

We Need a Healer

Jesus, we need a healer.
We need You to heal us.
Jesus, You healed the lepers
And You also healed the blind.

We know how to heal the lepers,
But we don't know how to heal the blind.
Jesus, we need your power
To open the blind people's eyes.

Jesus, they are blind and can't see You,
They can't see what you have done.
Jesus, they don't know about You,
They don't know that You and your Father act as one.

Jesus, our spirits, the same as our eyes, can go blind.
Help people with blinded spirits to be healed with your might.
Give us your love and wisdom,
Heal our spirits, the same as our eyes.

Only by restoring people's blindness,
A proper work can be done,
Jesus, only with your love and kindness,
People of the world can unite as one.

My Lord

In the love of people,
I recognize you.
In the eyes of children,
I see you.
My Lord and my God.

At the sight of mountains,
I worship you.
In the sound of the wind,
I hear you.
My Lord and my God.

At the sight of the sky,
I see your might.
At the sight of the sea,
I feel a fright.
My Lord and my God.

At the time of prayer,
I feel you.
A the time of crying,
I long for you.
My Lord and my God.

At the time of dying,
I will need you.
At the time of death,
I will come to you.
My Lord and my God.

Prayer to the Trinity

In the name of the Father,
The Son,
And the Holy Spirit,
Amen.

Father above me,
Son beside me,
Holy Spirit in me,
All three stay with me.

Three in one,
God in three persons,
Blessed Trinity,
All three dwell in me.

God the Father love me,
God the Son guide me,
God the Spirit advise me,
All three hear me.

Holy Trinity, bless me,
Holy Trinity, protect me,
Holy Trinity, teach me,
Holy Trinity, help me.

Three always was,
Three always is,
Three will always be.
God is unity.

God's Plan

God created us for Himself,
We belong to Him.
He lets us live here on earth,
And gives us a free will.

This free will leads us astray,
Away from God's will.
But God's will is essential,
We should always listen just to Him.

God has a plan for His people,
And because of His plan we are here.
We should not change His creation,
And with His plan we should not interfere.

We should increase our knowledge
About His will here on earth.
We should be brave and have courage,
To learn about what God's will say.

God's Love

God, your nature is so beautiful.
God, your nature is so pure.
God, your nature is so inspiring,
It shows that your love for us will endure.

We know that You love us, God,
But we disobey You still.
We know that You love us, God,
But we don't want to do your will.

We are arrogant and proud.
You gave us a free will.
You don't want us to be your puppets,
You want us to have our own zeal.

God, we know that You are the Master of the Universe,
Our knowledge about it is clear.
We know that You govern the sky and the earth,
And that all of us are dear.

We know all that, but we still don't listen,
We disobey and rebel.
But You forgive us and love us,
You don't send us straight to hell.

You have patience with us God, You give us chances.
You respect our free will.
We don't deserve your forgiveness.
We should all pay our bill.

Longing for God's Love

There is longing in a human heart
That never goes away.
No matter how poor or rich we are
The longing will always stay.

There is a longing in a human heart
That people can't comprehend.
It is a burning in their souls
That doesn't seem to end.

People are longing for God's love,
Love we search for but don't come about.
The love that's there, but can't be found,
The love that can be found if there is no doubt.

But we are doubting, not believing,
That God loves us and wants us saved.
We are doubting, not believing,
In the words that Jesus claimed.

We will find the love we long for.
We will find it if we try.
To find God's love is not easy,
It needs courage, trust and to know why.

We need to know why we are longing,
We need to know that we need this drive.
We were created in His image,
He shows His way for which we strive.

The Longing

We are longing for You Lord,
We are longing everywhere.
No matter how rich or poor we are,
The longing is still there.

It is a longing that we don't understand,
It is a longing that has no end.
It is a longing of a human heart,
A heart that our Creator had made.

The people are trying to satisfy this longing,
With riches and with fame,
But this longing can only be satisfied,
If we believe in You and know your name.

Without believing in You, Lord,
This longing we can't explain.
Only by coming to You, Lord,
This longing will end for us one day.

What a Great Love

Jesus, don't let me to forget about you.
Jesus, don't forget about me.
Jesus, you know that I love you.
I know what you did for us, by dying on a tree.

You died on a cross
Made out of a tree.
You suffered for us,
You died for me.

Why don't we all remember
That you have chosen a cross
To bring us with you to heaven?
That you have suffered and died.
That you have chosen both.

What a great love it has to be,
If God becomes a man.
If he dies comes down from heaven.
If he dies for us, so that we can live again.

On Love

You always love us, Jesus,
And your love is in me.
You always love us, Jesus,
And that is what will always be.

You don't want us to be angry,
You don't want us to get mad.
We killed you Jesus for your love.
That is not what you deserved.

You told us to be hopeful,
The fear is hard to bear.
You told us not to be afraid,
The fear can bring us to despair.

You know, Jesus, that we are weak.
You want to make us strong.
Your teachings will help us to love.
Your love will guide us to where we belong.

Stop Fighting

God is the light that shines bright,
God is the truth that is right,
God is the way we want to find.
He said, "Follow me and stop the fight".

To stop the fight is essential,
God should be known everywhere.
There are still people that don't know Him,
Those people are still here and there.

He wants us to love each other,
He wants us to love our enemies.
His teachings should stop the fighting,
We have known that for centuries.

We don't believe in His teaching,
We don't find truth where it is.
Only seeing is believing,
For the human race as it is.

God can't be seen, but we can know Him
From His teaching and what He has done.
Human beings won't stop fighting
Until God sends His Son.

His Son will come to stop the fighting,
God doesn't want to lose this race.
We don't know that we are starting
To lose His patience and His grace.

God and His People

Men who fly around the earth and sky
Don't know that they are mine.
I created both of them,
They both belong to My "Big Plan".

The plan is not yours, it is mine.
I will control the earth and sky.
You can't pollute the air and earth,
Don't make me send a curse.

I gave people a free will,
But with pollution you will pay the bill.
Don't you see what you have created?
Do you really think this can be debated?

I sent you the prophets, I sent you my Son,
But your change of minds was not yet done.
You talk about My Son, you like that he has come,
But you don't respect that he and I are one.

I love you and can change my mind,
If you will listen and come to my side.
Listen to the prophets, listen to my word.
Don't ignore all that you have heard.

Preachers

World needs people who are holy,
World needs people who can pray.
Not in churches, but God's nature,
Where people pray, God will stay.

Priests, ministers and preachers,
We heard enough of what they say.
It is always the same story,
The same story every day.

They should listen to God's teachings,
They should find Him where He is.
They should listen to the people,
They don't listen to the way it is.

We need people who are holy,
That can teach us every day
About God's laws and His calling,
We should listen to what they say.

The way preachers talk to people
Doesn't touch the heart or mind.
It is the duty of all preachers
To be holy with God in mind.

God is with us, He is patient,
He allows us time to learn
About His love and His teachings,
We have His love and life to earn.

The Designer

God, You created the atom, the molecules and the cells.
You created a wonder in the cell itself.
God, we are only duplicating
What you have already done yourself.

God, we have to further study the cell's design,
So that we can see what has already been done,
So that we can see the elegance of your design,
So that we can see from where life has come.

We have to see that life has come from a creator,
We have to see that God is the core of everything.
We have to admit who is the designer
Of the world and every little thing.

God, the technology is already in the cell.
The highly efficient organization in cells has a fine-tuning,
The evidence of You as the Creator is strongly present.
The knowledge of You as the Creator is re-assuring.

God's Will

To do God's will is essential.
To know God's will is our task.
We should do his will always,
But to know how, we have to ask.

We should ask God to help us
To recognize his will.
To put us on the proper path,
To put us there is up to Him.

If we will ask and try to be proper,
His will comes to pass.
He will help us to go through it,
It will become our task.

To know God's will is not easy,
We don't sometimes understand.
We are trying to do God's will,
But our doubts have to end.

We have to stay still and listen,
We should not be afraid.
He would help us if we ask Him.
We will be happy at the end.

The Power of God

God is the Creator
He gave us a free will.
God is the Power,
We should comply with Him.

God is the Wisdom
We should listen to Him.
God can instruct us
If we will pray to Him.

God's Hand can protect us
If we will love Him.
God's shield will defend us
If we will let Him.

Host of God will guard us
If it will be our will.
He has the strength to pilot us,
He can protect us from the sin.

With God's love we will be protected
Against the snares of evil in this world.
With God's love we will be protected
Against the temptations that lay ahead.

God's Nature

God, Your nature is so beautiful;
The mountains, the trees, the waters and all that grows.
God, your creatures are so colourful;
Man can see your wonders wherever he goes.

God, why can't we agree that You are the Creator,
Why do we think that creation was by chance?
Why are our eyes and minds so blinded?
Not to see your wonders at the very glance?

The wonders of your creation, God, are everywhere,
But we don't get it, we just stare.
We think that it was all accidental;
There is a lot of knowledge with you to share.

We have scientists that just can't get it,
They don't understand what you have done.
They can't get how all this fits together,
They can't believe that you are the only one.

All Religions

All religions of this world
Want people to have hope and to be saved.
All religions of this world
Want people to be happy and not sad.

Why do people fight in the name of religion?
Why do they kill? What is their vision?
There is only one God, who lived on this earth,
Who told us not to kill and who understands?

He understands our confusion in life;
He understands our problems and why we fight.
We should learn His teachings,
We should let Him be our guide.

People don't want to change religions,
People don't understand.
They follow their religion's vision
From the beginning to the end.

There is just one God in Heaven,
This God can understand.
He gives us a chance to know Him;
He can help us get to the happy end.

Two Ways

All religions in the world
Help people to be good and listen to what God said.
People need religion when in despair.
People pray to someone who should be there.

Why do people fight in the name of religion?
Why do they kill, what is their vision?
There is one God, who lived on this earth
Who told us not to kill, not to bring on the curse.

This God gave us the rules, he understands.
He wants to teach us, to bring us to the happy ends.
He is the God who cares.
He is the God who opened the heavens first.

Many people sing the glory to the living God,
While others offer their lives to the devil's plot.
God wants to bring us to freedom that lies ahead,
But the devil is determined to bring us to bondage at the end.

There are only two ways we can go;
One to the right to follow the glow and one to the left down below.
The way to the right is not easy, it takes courage.
The way to the left makes us sin for which we will be punished.

We have to be on guard if we want to be saved.
"Follow me, I am the way", is what this God said.
"You should not have other Gods than Me,
I lived among you and showed you on which side to be."

The Prayer in the Garden

You were always a part of the Trinity,
But you came down to Earth;
And you came to be with us, Jesus,
To bear the agony of death.

At your final hours here on Earth,
You went to the garden.
You went there with your friends,
You prayed for us to be pardoned.

You returned from the prayer,
Your friends were asleep.
You said, "The mind is willing,
But the body is weak."

Our bodies are weak
Because they are made up of flesh,
But our minds will survive,
Beyond the hour of our death.

Your teachings are powerful, Jesus,
They nurture us more than bread.
If we want to come to you
We have to listen to what you said.

"Not only by bread the man is living,
But by every word that God said",
You are the one who is forgiving,
The loads of sins that bring our death.

On Power

God, we need your power
For our intentions are weak.
Our willpower can't always resolve
What our lives so desperately need.

The power of God can resolve
What our greed has created.
The power of God can help us to do
What our hate has prevented.

Our hate keeps us from peace
While our greed prevents our happiness.
We need your power, our Merciful God,
We need your power here and abroad.

The nations are trying to destroy each other
Instead of helping and working together.
If You won't help us, God,
We will destroy the earth.

If you won't help us, God, who will be with You in the universe?

The One Who Always Was

You are the one who was predicted,
You are the one who always was.
You were sent by your Father,
Your Father knew the cause.

You were the one who was expected,
You came to us by your own will.
You were the one who taught us,
You came to pay the bill.

You taught us to love each other,
You told us that heaven exists.
You were always the one with the Father,
You came to fulfill your Father's wish.

We have a free will that Father gave us,
We can love you or disobey.
The Father sent you to save us,
But we killed you the other day.

We don't understand how great you are,
We don't understand that you were a gift.
You were a gift from the Father,
Because of you, we continue to live.

We should thank you for dying for us,
For taking on human features.
You are the one that we should trust,
You chose to be always with us, Jesus.

The Calvary Hill

God gave us the Earth,
He gave us life,
The more he gave us
It was never enough.

We did not see his love,
We betrayed his trust,
We created a ransom,
It had to be paid by us.

The one who is His son
Was sent by Him,
To save us from damnation,
Now the future doesn't look so dim.

He agreed to save us
And to pay the bill,
Before He died for us
On Calvary Hill.

The Judgment Day

Why do people hurt each other?
Why don't they want to understand
That hurting their neighbour and their brother
Can bring them an unhappy end?

There are people that like hurting,
Those people like causing pain.
They use power to cause injustice,
For them, this is a game.

Those people forget about the judgment,
They forget about the judge.
They forget about the final calling,
The calling that is awaiting all of us.

They better think about it,
How much harm they have done
To their brother and their neighbour,
And if the harm can be undone.

When they will be called to their final judgment,
They can't undo what they have done.
They can't better their position,
They will be judged one by one.

It is too late at the final judgment,
It is too late if harm was done.
This judgment is for all people,
The judgment day will one day come.

Life on this earth is for a short time,
Our next life is forever.
If we stay guilty this time,
Then the time for repenting is never.

On Joy

God, only through You we can have joy,
The joy for which we strive.
Only you can give us the joy,
In exchange for our plight.

God, You are the Creator,
You fill our hearts with love.
Jesus told us not to worry,
That we will be alright.

We worry, Lord, when bad things happen,
We lose confidence in God.
We forget that You know our sorrow,
We forget that sorrow is our plot.

We forget that God is in control,
That only through You our confidence can grow.
You are with us always,
We are never alone.

To have confidence in God means our salvation,
We forget what You have done,
That we are a part of your creation,
That only through You our joy will come.

Seen and Unseen

I complained to mighty father,
I complained about you and me.
You could cure so many people,
If you would be here with me.

Father wants you to be with Him,
Father wants you to be saved.
He knows I will always love you,
I'll be with you at the end.

I don't know when the end is coming,
I talk to you every day.
My mind and heart is always with you,
You are with me when I pray.

I try to do things that will please you,
I know you watch me from above.
I wonder what you want me to do here,
I wonder if I do enough.

I fix my mind on what is unseen,
You taught me enough about that.
What is unseen is eternal,
I will see it, but not yet.

What is seen is temporary,
It has to stay here on earth.
We can't take it when we will leave,
Planet Earth for Universe.

Mother's Plea

Jesus, I pray to You,
I pray to You day and night,
I pray for your grace
To let my children see your might.

Jesus, they know about You
But your might, they cannot see.
Their love for You is lukewarm,
Show them your love the way You show it to me.

My plea to You, Jesus,
Is the same I always give.
I love my children, Jesus, so much,
It seems for them alone I live.

My plea to You, Jesus,
Is to keep them healthy and good.
I taught them about You,
I think I did what I could.

The times are changing, Jesus,
The influence of others sometimes is not good.
The children became adults,
I wanted them to always behave the best they could.

My heart is aching, Jesus,
They don't always show You their love as they should.
They are good people and they can do it,
If You help them Jesus, I think that they would.

Ava

My little darling Ava,
My granddaughter is here.
She has my dark blue eyes and her mother's smile,
I beam when she is near.

I love her stubbornness and her laughter,
My love for her is clear.
I like to kiss her little curls,
Everything about her is dear.

She likes to imitate the adults,
But in age, she is not even two.
She can talk, say rhymes, likes to count,
She must have a high I.Q.

She can dance and sing and perform.
She knows the pictures in the books.
I know when she is happy or sad,
I love to see her curious looks.

There is so much I expect from Ava,
I hope I will still be here
When Ava grows into a beautiful woman;
When she comes to see me and be near.

My Grandchildren

My grandchildren are presents from heaven,
They are the encouragement that I need.
This takes away my sorrow
So I forget about my grief.

To be with them is a blessing,
They bring me a lot of joy.
When I am with them I see a new life,
It's a pleasure to watch them grow.

They are little darlings
With innocent little souls.
They mean so much to all of us,
It is to them where our duty goes.

To ensure them their future,
To be responsible for their lives,
To love them and protect them,
Will always be our task.

My children are their parents,
They should always be there for them.
My grandchildren need their parents' love,
Without it, their lives won't be the same.

Parent's Advice

Parent's advice is seldom appreciated,
The child's respect is hard to get.
Parent's advice is directed by the heart,
The child's answer is, "not yet".

When the children become parents,
They will start to understand
That their mother and their father
Want to bring them to a happy end.

The children's answer to the advice
Will often be, "no, no, no",
Though a mother's love and father's firmness
Will bring the child on the right path to go.

As trees have to be pruned early
To keep them from growing wild,
So children need to be corrected early
To keep them from falling behind.

If the child won't be corrected,
It will think that it is right.
Its ignorance will keep on growing
And its future won't be bright.

Drowning

The two-year old lad
Walked to the lake alone.
Wandered away from his friends,
We did not notice that he was gone.

The little curious guy
Wanted to explore.
He wandered to the dock,
He wanted to learn more.

He remembered to jump into his mother's arms,
When she taught him to swim.
He jumped into the lake,
But his mother was not there for him.

The lake was deep.
The water was cold.
He could not swim.
He could not float.

Where is my mother?
Why is she not here?
But the guardian angel was standing by.
The guardian angel was the one who was near.

The guardian angel
Helped the toddler fight,
To keep his head above the water,
To fight for his life.

His loved ones had noticed
That the lad was gone.
They saw him in the water,
He was alone no more.

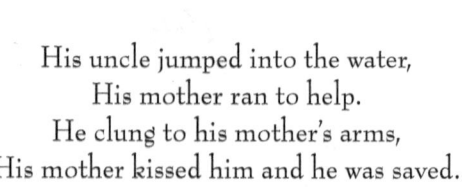

His uncle jumped into the water,
His mother ran to help.
He clung to his mother's arms,
His mother kissed him and he was saved.

Thank you Lord All Mighty
For saving my grandson's life,
For letting us know
About the little guys fright.

The Spoiled Son

When a son was born to a father,
His father wanted his son to excel.
He wanted him to be better than others.
He wanted his son to be better than himself.

The father wanted to be proud of his son,
But his son did not understand.
His son got into all kinds of trouble
That brought the father shame in the end.

The father believed and tried harder.
He thought his son understood,
But the son was stubborn and did not care.
The father hit him and the son struck him as hard as he could.

There was no need for the fighting
Between the father and the son.
If only the father would realize
How much he was spoiling his beloved son.

To My Sister-in-Law

We, whose lives you touched, cry for you.
We loved you, but you did not know about it.
We, whose lives you were a part of, look for you.
We look for the way you left, but we did not find it.

You were the one who never confirmed.
You were the one who like to rebel.
You were the one who liked to go ahead.
You were the one who liked to excel.

If we had told you that we love you,
You would not have believed us.
If we had told you that we like to be with you,
Would you have left us?

You were a free spirit,
You liked to be free.
You did not like to listen to us,
You did not want help from me.

I did not know that I would miss you so much,
I miss you now when you are gone.
I always admired your courage,
You did not mind being alone.

You did not seem to be discouraged
When things did not go your way.
You did not need to be encouraged
To try new ways of life again.

You always did what you wanted,
You did not take anybody's advice.
You wanted to be free and able to choose,
But you should accept the love as a gift from us.

The Stepmother

The child lost his mother at a tender age
Remembering her love.
The mother watched him every day,
Giving him love from above.

When the boy was four years old
His questions came around,
"My dearest father tell me please,
Where my mother can be found?"

"Your mother is sleeping a deep sleep,
Buried in a deep grave.
Nobody can wake her up,
Buried near the gate."

When the child heard from his father
Where his mother laid,
Running to the graveyard,
He found the grave and prayed.

Digging with his fingers,
Raking with his hand,
Digging deeper, deeper,
He could not get to the end.

The child cried for his mother,
And his mother heard his cry.
"Go home, my child, to your father,
He has found a new mother to stand by."

"The stepmother is not like you,
She does not put enough food on my plate.
When you were feeding me, my mother,
You were happy that I ate.

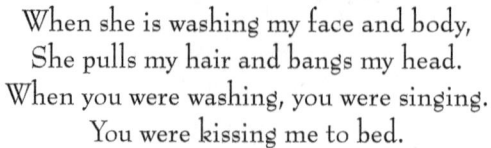

When she is washing my face and body,
She pulls my hair and bangs my head.
When you were washing, you were singing.
You were kissing me to bed.

My new mother doesn't like me,
She wishes I wasn't there.
Take me with you, dearest mother,
Take me into your care."

"Go home, my child, to your father,
I will take you in two days.
I won't leave you with your new mother,
She cannot take my place."

The first day, the child was ailing.
The second day, he was dead.
The third day, he was buried.
He found his true mother where he had been led.

The Orphan

The child lost his mother in infant's age,
Remembering her love.
He cried to get his mother back,
She heard him from above.

The child remembered his mother's touch,
He remembered her standing by.
He remembered her voice and laughter,
He remembered her lullaby.

The mother was sorry for her child,
And her spirit came to earth.
She brought her love back to her child,
She knew the child understands.

She came to the child at night,
She calmed his cry.
She put him gently to sleep
By singing a lullaby.

Sleep, sleep, my baby,
Have a nice dream.
Sleep, sleep, my baby,
Your mother is near.

When the night comes,
Then I shall be here,
Don't worry, my baby,
I will be near.

Sleep, sleep, my baby,
Sleep the whole night,
When the sun comes,
The sky will be bright.

The Lavender Bush

The mother died, was put to rest
While her children stayed behind.
Each morning before they ate their bread,
They searched for where their mother could be found.

They knew their mother's lavender scent,
That scent was all around.
They searched her room and her bed,
But their mother could not be found.

The mother heard her children's cries
And her soul came back to Earth.
She wanted children to come by
And find her place of rest.

She changed into a lavender bush
On the place where she rests.
She wanted to know if her children would come,
She put her children to the test.

The children found the lavender bush,
They knew their mother was standing by.
And that little lavender bush
Was the only one that could calm their cry.

Picking Blueberries

At Tamagami wilderness,
Where a little island is,
You let me pick up blueberries
While you wanted to catch a fish.

I did not want to stay without you,
I did not want the fish.
I wanted to be beside you,
I wanted you to bring me a full dish.

You wandered away from me,
To pick blueberries was too much to ask.
You wanted to go and be free,
To catch a fish was your task.

You wandered away to pick blueberries,
You wanted to fulfill my wish.
I could not see you through the trees.
I looked for you and fell into a ditch.

I got scared and called you back,
My voice was in high pitch.
I asked you why you went away,
You showed me an empty dish.

You said you went to find the big ones,
Those that you saw were too small.
I had to laugh, I saw my mistake,
I had to let you go.

You were happy to be free
And went to catch a fish.
You caught the fish and came back to me
And we both had a feast.

Clearing in the Woods

There is a clearing in the woods
Where the path leads so high.
There is a clearing in the woods
Where we went, you and I.

The bear is walking with her cubs,
There in the clearing without doubts.
There in the clearing with no fear
That you and I will see her cubs.

There is a clearing in the woods
Where you and I used to go,
Where deer and fawns are running free,
Where wild flowers and ferns grow.

There is so much light in that clearing,
Which you can't see in the woods,
Where the raspberries and mushrooms grow,
Where there is pasture for the moose.

We picked up raspberries and mushrooms too,
In the clearing where the morning's dew
Left drops of moisture on moss that grew
Beneath the trees which we knew.

We watched the trees, how high they grow!
We picked up mushrooms there below
And watched the stream flow
To the lake where most streams go.

The Deer is Coming

The sun is shining,
The ice is breaking,
The spring is coming here.
The snow is melting,
The deer is coming near.

The deer is finding little birches,
They are getting some sweet sap.
The deer will know where to find it,
The birches will snap, snap, snap.

The little birches won't have a chance
To grow into a tree.
All the deer is thinking,
Is just me, me, me.

If he can't find the little birches,
He will eat a little cedar tree.
That is also a good snacking,
For the deer who thinks, "Me, me, me".

Poor little trees can't run away,
The deer had a delicious snack.
The deer is doing this year by year,
He is always coming back.

Going Fishing

There was a morning dew,
When we stepped into the boat.
There was a fog surrounding you and me,
When we went fishing at six o'clock.

I was scared; I did not want to go.
There was a fog on the lake
But you insisted that we should go,
To catch a fish, in the lake below.

We could not see where we were going,
We could not see the fishing line.
We could not see the lake through the dew,
I was scared, but for you it was fine.

You were happy and laughing,
You did not know that I was scared.
The lake was quiet and it was calming
Even though we could not see ahead.

We caught a fish and you were happy,
You wanted to catch one more.
I was tired and sleepy
But you were alert and ready to go.

The Fisherman and the Fish

The lake is calm, the day is about to start.
It is a quiet Sunday morning.
Dawn has come with mist around,
The fisherman is yawning.

He has no rest, he has to go.
He has to catch a fish.
He knows the place where the fish go,
His boat is waiting at the beach.

Its morning time, the fish go by.
They want to have a feast.
The fisherman has enough bait
To catch a lot of fish.

Some fish are smart, they choose their bite.
They know what to eat.
The fisherman will try and try
To satisfy his wish.

Some fish are starving, they bite and bite.
They bite without fear.
The lake is calm, the fish swim around.
The fisherman is near.

The fish will bite, the hook will cut.
The fish is on the line.
The fish will fight, it will not bite.
The fisherman has won.

The Outdoors

The outdoor life was what you liked, my darling
All your life, most of all.
You liked to work outside, to construct,
You liked the plants and watched them grow.

You liked to travel and explore,
You liked the nature and the wilderness.
You liked to get up before the sun,
You were an adventurist.

In winter, you liked ice fishing,
You did not mind waiting in the cold for fish.
You knew how to get a fish on your line,
For you, catching fish was a bliss.

You liked cross country skiing and snowshoeing,
Through the woods and across the frozen lake.
To be outside for you was a blessing
Even if your life was at stake.

You were full of life and energy,
You were a picture of health.
Until one day a mystery
Brought your dreams and life to an end.

The Well in the Woods

I know the place where the spring is crystal clear,
Where the spring makes a well,
Where ferns grow and the deer are near,
Where birds nest and squirrels dwell.

The deer come to drink from the well at night,
When everything is calm.
The birds come to drink when it is light,
To sing songs and hum.

The birds and deer, they all come near,
Near the spring which makes a well.
They all come to the well to drink,
They all know the way.

When all is calm and the moon is bright,
The stars shine on the well.
The well is like a mirror's side,
Reflecting the moon and the stars as well.

When woods sleep and all is calm
And the stars and moon shine clear,
The stars and moon are like golden charms.
The well is like a golden beam.

The Invasion

It was like thunder that woke us up that night,
The tanks roared ahead and around.
Big metal monsters came about,
The tanks were shaking our country's ground.

"This little country is the heart of Europe,
You have your own vast land," we said.
"Why did you come here?
It is not your land."

Who will help us?
There is no help ahead.
"You will serve and listen to us,"
That is what they said.

We have heard about a country,
That lay in a distant land.
That country wants to take us.
It will take those who fled.

Three travelers left their beloved land.
Who is that little crying lad?
It was their country
That the travelers left.

The Time I Don't Forget

It was a long time ago,
It was in nineteen sixty eight,
The time we came to this country,
The time I don't forget.

It was the time when my country was occupied,
When many people fled.
It was the time that is forgotten,
But not by us who lived through that.

A monster with soldiers, tanks, bullets and terror,
Came to my beloved land.
They had no grounds and it was not in error,
They occupied my country and they stayed.

They put people into prisons,
They made us into their slaves,
If you would speak, it was treason,
You would go in, under the gates.

To get out of the country was not easy,
But few of us managed that,
We were allowed to go on breathing,
The air of a free and prosperous land.

God, please save this land from totalitarian horror,
Save this land from hatred, suffering, death and genocide,
Let this land be run by wise people,
Where ruthless regimes will have no ground.

Three Travelers from a Distant Land

They were travelers from a distant land,
Without money, without water, without bread.
Two travelers and a little lad;
Three foreigners from a foreign land.

Why did they come here?
This is not their land.
From far away
The three travelers fled.

From a country they both loved,
From parents who loved them.
Why did they decide to come?
Who is the one to blame?

Their land was taken,
It will never be the same.
Their land was occupied
By the one who was to blame.

They thought about their future
And forgot about the rest.
They did not know the people,
But did what they thought was the best.

It was not their language,
The new one that they have heard.
It was not their roof under which they rest,
Three travelers came to a foreign land.

The Enemies

Governments are making problems,
They don't protect life and peace.
They allow changing nature,
They don't stop the enemies.

Enemies are getting richer,
Honest people must work hard.
Enemies are changing the crops,
Making money is their task.

To be rich is not important,
To be healthy is the aim.
It's the aim for people that are honest,
But rich people think it's a game.

The cows are being fed protein,
Which the cows should never eat.
We are drinking milk from those cows
To whom only grain and grass we should feed.

We are quiet, we don't protest.
We let them do what they want.
They don't ask us if they can do it,
We should put them all on hold.

Enemies make breathing harder,
They are cutting our trees.
Oxygen is getting lower,
Who will blame the enemies?

Governments can save the nature
By using sun and wind instead of gas.
Governments should stop the damage,
Both to nature and to us.

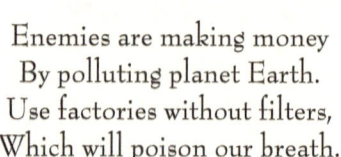

Enemies are making money
By polluting planet Earth.
Use factories without filters,
Which will poison our breath.

They don't ask us if we agree
For them to change our crops.
They grow crops that bugs will not eat,
We are the one's who will suffer most.

Why are crops genetically altered?
They don't ask us if it's okay,
If they can change God's nature.
For them it's the money game.

Our food chain has been altered,
It is making us all ill.
Governments are doing nothing,
They don't hear our reasoning and will.

Who will raise voice and tell the government,
To use the power that they have.
Who will stop enemies from getting richer,
On the account of our dead?

If we will not stop polluting
Our bodies and the Earth,
God won't help us save the planet.
"I gave you free will," He said.

People Of Mutual Love

Blessed are the people of mutual love,
That can conquer hate and fright.
Their love will help them to be just,
And build friendships that can last.

Blessed are the people that seek peace,
They can see what the world needs.
People like them can open their minds and hearts
To those who have been hurt and have cried.

People of mutual love should be heard,
Their song of peace to be shared.
They can give us a hope that nobody has heard
And because of their love, the word can be saved.

The peace can teach people to be kind,
With peace, people can try to be loved.
Peace will let love flow,
And with love, everything can grow.

The Hate

If your neighbour makes you suffer,
If he brings hatred to your name,
You still have to think of him as your brother.
You should not hate him and be the same.

If you stay calm and silent,
The hate will come back to him and stay.
He will be ashamed for what he has done,
There will be no ground for his play.

If you get mad and hate him,
You will agree with his game.
He will be happy that he could hurt you
And he will try to hurt you again.

It is not easy to feel love
For the person who only shows hate,
But if you will stay calm and won't react
He, one day, will regret.

Young People Need Direction

Jesus, young people thirst for wisdom,
They need someone to imitate,
They need your wisdom and kindness,
To be good people at the end.

Young people are lost at the crossroads,
They don't know which way to turn.
One way will make them go the right direction,
The other way will make them go astray.

They can't go in both directions,
They can choose only one way.
If they choose the wrong direction,
Bad influence can come and stay.

The wrong way will make them wicked,
But it has a great appeal,
They can lose their souls on it,
But they are young and have zeal.

Jesus, help them with your kindness,
Jesus, help them with your love,
Jesus, you can make great wonders,
With your power from above.

The Oasis

To have an oasis is important,
Everybody should have one.
That's where we go in times of crisis,
You can think about all you have done.

It is a place where we can worship.
It is a place where we can pray.
It is a place where we can weep.
It is a place where we can stay.

An oasis can be just a small place,
Outside or in a home.
An oasis is not for other people,
An oasis is our own.

Rest Body and Soul

When you are tired and feeling weary,
Rest your body as a whole.
Because your thoughts can be contrary
To the thoughts of a rested soul.

Your body and soul get tired,
They need to rejuvenate.
You need to rest and stay silent,
You will feel stronger at the end.

The soul gets tired, the body gets weak.
The soul and body are a union.
If your body feels tired and weary
Your thoughts will be thoughts of a tired soul.

After you rest in silence
Your body and soul will be ready to go.
You will feel strong and patient,
You will feel your thoughts glow.

So remember that rest is important,
The soul and body act like one.
Remember that if you are tired
Your thoughts will let you down.

On Metamorphosis

The same as the caterpillar,
Discards his cocoon and can fly,
You discarded your earthly body,
And received a body from the Most High.

The same as the caterpillar,
Gets his wings to go by,
The same you got a new body,
And you can now reach the sky.

Metamorphosis of the caterpillar,
Which transformation lets him fly,
Is like metamorphosis of your body,
Which transformation can be divine.

The caterpillar discards the cocoon,
And he can fly high,
You discarded your earthly body,
And received the body that will never die.

The caterpillar sheds his body,
The butterfly's home is the sky,
But where is your home now, my darling,
It is no more the same as mine.

I know where butterflies go sleeping,
I know where butterflies can go,
I know that you had to leave me here,
But where you went, I do not know.

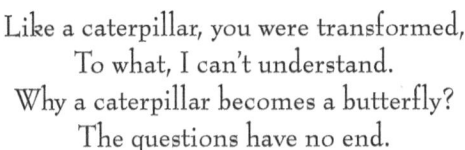

Like a caterpillar, you were transformed,
To what, I can't understand.
Why a caterpillar becomes a butterfly?
The questions have no end.

You come to me through closed doors,
You talk to me at night,
You put the light for me to see,
You let me see God's might.